The Book of Church Order of the Presbyterian Church in the United States

THE BOOK

OF

CHURCH ORDER,

OF

THE PRESBYTERIAN CHURCH

IN

THE UNITED STATES.

Adopted 1879.

RICHMOND, VA.:
Presbyterian Committee of Publication.
ST. LOUIS:
Presbyterian Publishing Co.

PART I.

FORM OF GOVERNMENT.

CHAPTER I.

OF THE DOCTRINE OF CHURCH GOVERNMENT.

I. The scriptural form of church government, which is that of Presbytery, is comprehended under these five heads of doctrine —viz: 1. Of the Church ; 2. Of its members; 3. Of its officers; 4. Of its courts; and 5. Of its orders.

II. The Church which the Lord Jesus Christ has erected in this world for the gathering and perfecting of the saints, is His visible kingdom of grace, and is one and the same in all ages.

III. The members of this visible Church catholic are all those persons in every nation, together with their children, who make profession of the holy religion of Christ, and of submission to His laws.

IV. The officers of the Church, by whom all its powers are administered, are, according to the Scriptures, Ministers of the Word, Ruling Elders, and Deacons.

V. Ecclesiastical jurisdiction is not a several, but a joint power to be exercised by Presbyters in courts. These courts may have

5

jurisdiction over one or many churches; but they sustain such mutual relations as to realize the idea of the unity of the Church.

VI. The ordination of officers is ordinarily by a court.

VII. This scriptural doctrine of Presbytery is necessary to the perfection of the order of the visible Church, but is not essential to its existence.

CHAPTER II.

OF THE CHURCH.

Section I.—Of its King and Head.

I. Jesus Christ, upon whose shoulders the government is, whose name is called Wonderful, Counsellor, the Mighty God, the Everlasting Father, the Prince of Peace; of the increase of whose government and peace there shall be no end; who sits upon the throne of David, and upon his kingdom, to order it and to establish it with judgment and with justice from henceforth, even forever; having all power given unto Him in heaven and in earth by the Father, who raised Him from the dead, and set Him on His own right hand, far above all principality and power, and might, and dominion, and every name that is named, not only in this world, but also in that which is to come, and hath put all things under His feet, and gave Him to be the Head over all things to the Church, which is His body, the fullness of Him that filleth all in all; He being ascended up far above all heavens, that He might fill all things. received gifts for His Church, and gave all officers necessary for the edification of His Church, and the perfecting of His saints.

II. Jesus, the Mediator, the sole Priest, Prophet, King, Saviour, and Head of the Church, contains in Himself, by way of eminency, all the offices in His Church, and has many of their names attributed to Him in the Scriptures. He is Apostle, Teacher, Pastor, Minister and Bishop, and the only Lawgiver in Zion. It belongs to His Majesty from His throne of glory, to rule and teach the Church, through His Word and Spirit, by the ministry of men; thus mediately exercising His own authority, and enforcing His own laws, unto the edification and establishment of His kingdom.

III. Christ as King, has given to His Church, officers, oracles and ordinances; and especially has He ordained therein His system of doctrine, government, discipline, and worship; all which are either expressly set down in Scripture, or by good and necessary consequence may be deduced therefrom; and to which things He commands that nothing be added, and that from them naught to be taken away.

IV. Since the ascension of Jesus Christ to heaven, He is present with the Church by His Word and Spirit, and the benefits of all His offices are effectually applied by the Holy Ghost.

Section II.—The Visible Church Defined.

I. The visible Church before the law, under the law, and now under the gospel, is one and the same, and consists of all those who make profession of the true religion, together with their children.

II. This visible unity of the body of Christ, though obscured, is not destroyed by its division into different denominations of professing Christians; but all of these which maintain the word and sacraments in their fundamental integrity are to be recognized as true branches of the Church of Jesus Christ.

III. It is according to scriptural example that the Church should be divided into many particular churches.

Section III.—Of the Nature and Extent of Church Power.

I. The power which Christ has committed to His Church vests in the whole body, the rulers and the ruled, constituting it a spiritual commonwealth. This power, as exercised by the people, extends to the choice of those officers whom He has appointed in His Church.

II. Ecclesiastical power, which is wholly spiritual, is two-fold: the officers exercise it sometimes severally, as in preaching the gospel, administering the sacraments, reproving the erring, visiting the sick, and comforting the afflicted, which is the power of order; and they exercise it sometimes jointly in Church courts, after the form of judgment, which is the power of jurisdiction.

III. The sole functions of the Church, as a kingdom and government distinct from the civil commonwealth, are to proclaim, to administer, and to enforce the law of Christ revealed in the Scriptures.

IV. The Church, with its ordinances, officers, and courts, is the agency which Christ has ordained for the edification and government of His people, for the propagation of the faith, and for the evangelization of the world.

V. The exercise of ecclesiastical power, whether joint or several, has the divine sanction, when in conformity with the statutes enacted by Christ, the Lawgiver, and when put forth by courts or by officers appointed thereunto in His word.

Section IV.—Of the Particular Church.

I. A particular church consists of a number of professing Christians, with their offspring, associated together for divine worship and godly living, agreeably to the Scriptures, and submitting to the lawful government of Christ's kingdom.

II. Its officers are the Pastor, the Ruling Elders, and the Deacons.

III Its jurisdiction being a joint power, is lodged in the hands of the church session, consisting of the Pastor and Ruling Elders.

IV. To the Deacons belongs the administration of the offerings for the poor and other pious uses. To them, also may be properly committed the charge of the temporal affairs of the church.

V. The ordinances established by Christ, the Head, in His Church are, prayer; singing praises: reading, expounding, and preaching the Word of God; administering the sacraments of baptism and the Lord's Supper; public solemn fasting and thanksgiving; catechising; making offerings for the relief of the poor, and for other pious uses; exercising discipline; and blessing the people.

VI. Churches destitute of the official ministrations of the Word ought not therefore, to forsake the assembling of themselves together, but should be convened by the Session on the Lord's day and at other suitable times for prayer, praise, the reading of the Holy Scriptures, and exhortation, or the reading of a sermon of some approved minister. In like manner, Christians whose lot is cast in destitute regions ought to meet for the worship of God.

Section V.—Of the Organization of a Particular Church.

I. In the organization of a church, the first step shall be to receive testimonials on behalf of such of the applicants as are members of the Church, if there be any ; and then to admit upon a profession of faith in Christ such candidates as on examination may be found qualified.

II. These persons should, in the next place, be required to enter into covenant, by answering the following questions affirmatively, with the uplifted hand, viz : "Do you, in reliance on God for strength, solemnly promise and covenant that you will walk together as an organized church, on the principles of the faith and order of the Presbyterian Church, and that you will study the purity and harmony of the whole body?" The presiding minister shall then say : "I now pronounce and declare that you are constituted a church, according to the Word of God and the faith and order of the Presbyterian Church in the United States. In the name of the Father, and of the Son, and of the Holy Ghost. Amen."

III. Ruling Elders and Deacons are then to be elected, ordained and installed.

CHAPTER III.

OF CHURCH MEMBERS.

I. The infant seed of believers are, through the covenant and by right of birth, members of the Church. Hence, they are entitled to baptism, and to the pastoral oversight, instruction, and government of the Church, with a view to their embracing Christ, and thus possessing personally all the benefits of the covenant.

II. All baptized persons are entitled to the watchful care, instruction and government of the Church, even though they are adults and have made no profession of faith in Christ.

III. Those only who have made a profession of faith in Christ are entitled to all the rights and privileges of the Church.

CHAPTER IV.

OF CHURCH OFFICERS.

Section I.—Of their General Classification.

I. Under the New Testament, our Lord at first collected His people out of different nations. and united them to the household of faith by the mission of extraordinary officers, endued with miraculous gifts, which have long since ceased.

II. The whole polity of the Church consists in doctrine, government, and distribution. And the ordinary and perpetual officers in the Church are, Teaching Elders, or Ministers of the Word, who are commissioned to preach the gospel and administer the sacraments. and also to rule ; Ruling Elders, whose office is to wait on government; and Deacons, whose function is the distribution of the offerings of the faithful for pious uses.

III. No one who holds office in the Church ought to usurp authority therein, or receive any official titles of spiritual pre-eminence, except such as are employed in the Scriptures.

Section II.—Of the Minister of the Word.

I. This office is the first in the Church, both for dignity and usefulness. The person who fills it has in Scripture different titles expressive of his various duties. As he has the oversight of the flock of Christ, he is termed Bishop. As he feeds them with spiritual food, he is termed Pastor. As he serves Christ in His Church, he is termed Minister. As it is his duty to be grave and prudent, and an example to the flock, and to govern well in the house and kingdom of Christ, he is termed Presbyter or Elder. As he is the messenger of God, he is termed Angel of the Church. As he is sent to declare the will of God to sinners, and to beseech them to be reconciled to God through Christ, he is termed Ambassador. As he bears the glad tidings of salvation to the ignorant and perishing, he is termed Evangelist. As he stands to proclaim the gospel, he is termed Preacher. As he expounds the Word, and by sound doctrine both exhorts and convinces the gainsayer, he is termed Teacher. And as he dispenses the manifold grace of God, and the ordinances instituted by Christ, he is termed Steward of the mysteries of God. These titles do not indicate different grades of office, but all describe one and the same officer.

II. He that fills this office should possess **a** competency of human learning, and be blameless in life, sound in the faith, and apt to teach : he should exhibit a sobriety and holiness of conversation becoming the gospel ; he should rule his own house well : and should have **a** good report of them that are without.

III. As the Lord has given different gifts to the Ministers of the Word, and has committed to them various works to execute, the Church is authorized to call and appoint them to labour as Pastors, Teachers and Evangelists, and in such other works as may be needful to the Church, according to the gifts in which they excel.

IV. When a minister is called to labour as a Pastor, it belongs to his office to pray for and with his flock, as the mouth of the people unto God ; to feed the flock by reading, expounding and preaching the Word ; to direct the congregation in singing the praises of God ; to administer the sacraments ; to bless the people from God ; to catechise the children and youth ; to visit officially the people, devoting especial attention to the poor, the sick, the afflicted, and the dying ; and, with the other Elders, to exercise the joint power of government.

V. When a minister is appointed to be **a** teacher in a school of divinity, or to give instruction in the doctrines and duties of religion to youth assembled in a college or university, it appertains to his office to take a pastoral oversight of those committed to his charge, and be diligent in sowing the seed of the Word, and gathering the fruit thereof, as one who watches for souls.

VI. When a minister is appointed to the work of the Evangelist, he is commissioned to preach the Word and administer the sacraments in foreign countries, frontier settlements, or the destitute parts of the Church; and to him may be entrusted power to organize churches, and ordain Ruling Elders and Deacons therein.

VII. When a minister is called to labor through the press, or in any other like needful work, it shall be incumbent on him to make full proof of his ministry by disseminating the gospel for the edification of the Church.

Section III.—Of the Ruling Elder.

I. As there were in the Church, under the law, Elders of the people for the government thereof, so, in the gospel Church, Christ has furnished others besides the Ministers of the Word, with gifts and commission to govern when called thereunto, which officers are entitled Ruling Elders.

II. These Ruling Elders do not labor in the Word and doctrine, but possess the same authority in the courts of the Church as the Ministers of the Word.

III. Those who fill this office ought to be blameless in life and sound in the faith; they should be men of wisdom and discretion;

and by the holiness of their walk and conversation, should be examples to the flock.

IV. Ruling Elders, the immediate representatives of the people, are chosen by them, that, in conjunction with the Pastors or Ministers, they may exercise government and discipline, and take the oversight of the spiritual interests of the particular church, and also of the Church generally, when called thereunto. It appertains to their office, both severally and jointly, to watch diligently over the flock committed to their charge, that no corruption of doctrine or of morals enter therein. Evils which they cannot correct by private admonition, they should bring to the notice of the Session. They should visit the people at their homes, especially the sick; they should instruct the ignorant, comfort the mourner, nourish and guard the children of the Church; and all those duties which private Christians are bound to discharge by the law of charity are especially incumbent upon them by divine vocation, and are to be discharged as official duties. They should pray with and for the people; they should be careful and diligent in seeking the fruit of the preached word among the flock; and should inform the pastor of cases of sickness, affliction, and awakening, and of all others which may need his special attention.

Section IV.—Of the Deacon.

I. The office of Deacon is set forth in the Scriptures as ordinary and perpetual in the Church.

II. The duties of this office especially relate to the care of the poor, and to the collection and distribution of the offerings of the people for pious uses, under the direction of the Session. To the Deacons, also, may be properly committed the management of the temporal affairs of the Church,

III. To this office should be chosen men of honest repute and approved piety, who are esteemed for their prudence and sound judgment, whose conversation becomes the gospel, and whose lives are exemplary; seeing that those duties to which all Christians are called in the way of beneficence are especially incumbent on the Deacon as an officer in Christ's house.

IV. A complete account of collections and distributions, and a full record of proceedings shall be kept by the Deacons, and submitted to the Session for examination and approval at least once a year.

V. In churches where it is impossible to secure the appointment of a sufficient number of Deacons, the duties of this office devolve on the Ruling Elders.

VI. Where it shall appear needful, the church Session may select and appoint godly women for the care of the sick, of prisoners, of poor widows and orphans, and in general for the relief of distress.

CHAPTER V.

OF CHURCH COURTS:

Section I.—Of the Courts in General.

I. The Church is governed by various courts, in regular gradation; which are all, nevertheless, Presbyteries, as being composed exclusively of Presbyters.

II. These courts are church Sessions, Presbyteries. Synods, and the General Assembly.

III. The Pastor is Moderator of the session. The Moderator of the Presbytery, the Synod, and the General Assembly, shall be chosen at each stated meeting of these courts; and the Moderator, or in case of his absence, the last Moderator present, or, the oldest minister in attendance, shall open the next meeting with a sermon, unless it be highly inconvenient, and shall hold the chair until a new Moderator be chosen.

IV. The Moderator possesses all authority necessary for the preservation of order, and for convening and adjourning the court, according to its own ruling. He may also, on any extraordinary emergency, convene the court by his circular letter before the ordinary time of meeting. And in case of the failure of the appointed meeting, he may convene the court at a suitable time and place.

V. It is the duty of the Clerk, whose continuance in office shall be during the pleasure of the court, besides recording the transactions, to preserve the records carefully, and to grant extracts from them whenever properly required. Such extracts under the hand of the Clerk, shall be evidence to any ecclesiastical court, and to every part of the Church.

VI. Every meeting of the Presbytery, Synod and General Assembly shall be opened and closed with prayer; and in closing the final meeting, a psalm or hymn may be sung, and the benediction pronounced.

VII. The expenses of Ministers and Ruling Elders, in their attendance on the courts, shall be defrayed by the bodies which they respectively represent.

Section II. — Of the Jurisdiction of Church Courts.

I. These assemblies are altogether distinct from the civil magistracy, nor have they any jurisdiction in political or civil affairs. They have no power to inflict temporal pains and penalties; but their authority is in all respects moral or spiritual.

II. The jurisdiction of church courts is only ministerial and declarative, and relates to the doctrines and precepts of Christ, to the order of the Church, and to the exercise of discipline. *First,* they can make no laws binding the conscience; but may frame symbols of faith, bear testimony against error in doctrine and immorality in practice, within or without the pale of the Church, and decide cases of conscience. *Secondly,* they have power to establish rules for the government, discipline, worship, and extension of the Church, which must be agreeable to the doctrines relating thereto contained in the Scriptures, the circumstantial details only of these matters being left to the christian prudence and wisdom of church officers and courts. *Thirdly,* they possess the right of requiring obedience to the laws of Christ. Hence, they admit those qualified to sealing ordinances and to their respective offices; and they exclude the disobedient and disorderly from their offices, or from sacramental privileges; but the highest censure to which their authority extends, is to cut off the contumacious and impenitent from the congregation of believers. *Moreover,* they possess all the administrative authority necessary to give effect to these powers.

III. All church courts are one in nature, constituted of the same elements, possessed inherently of the same kinds of rights and powers, and differing only as the Constitution may provide. Yet it is according to scriptural example, and needful to the purity and harmony of the whole Church, that disputed matters of doctrine and order, arising in the lower courts, should be referred to the higher courts for decision.

IV. For the orderly and efficient dispatch of ecclesiastical business, it is necessary that the sphere of action of each court should be distinctly defined. The Session exercises jurisdiction over a single church; the Presbytery over what is common to the Ministers, Sessions and churches within a prescribed district; the Synod over what belongs in common to three or more Presbyteries, and their Ministers, Sessions and churches; and the General Assembly over such matters as concern the whole Church; and the jurisdiction of these courts is limited by the express provisions of the Constitution. Every court has the right to resolve questions of doctrine and discipline seriously and reasonably proposed, and in general to maintain truth and righteousness, condemning erroneous opinions and practices which tend to the injury of the peace, purity or progress of the Church; and although each court exercises exclusive original jurisdiction over all matters specially belonging to it, the lower courts are subject to the review and control of the higher courts, in regular gradation. Hence, these courts are not separate and independent tribunals;

but they have a mutual relation, and every act of jurisdiction is the act of the whole Church, performed by it through the appropriate organ.

Section III.—Of the Church Session.

I. The church Session consists of the Pastor or Pastors, if there be any, and the Ruling Elders of a church. Two Ruling Elders, if there be so many, with the Pastor, if there be one, shall be necessary to constitute a quorum.

II. In case of the absence of the Pastor, or when for prudential reasons it may appear advisable that some other Minister should preside, such Minister belonging to the same Presbytery, as the Pastor with the concurrence of the Elders may designate, shall be invited to preside in his place.

III. When a church is without a Pastor, the Moderator of the Session shall be either the Minister appointed for that purpose by the Presbytery, or one invited by the Session to preside on a particular occasion. But when it is inconvenient to procure the attendance of such a Moderator, the Session may proceed without it. In judicial cases this Moderator shall always be a member of the same Presbytery to which the church belongs.

IV. In churches where there are two or more Pastors, they shall, when present, alternately preside.

V. The church Session is charged with maintaining the spiritual government of the church, for which purpose it has power to inquire into the knowledge, principles and christian conduct of the church members under its care; to censure those found delinquent; to see that parents do not neglect to present their children for baptism; to receive members into the communion of the Church; to grant letters of dismission to other churches, which, when given to parents, shall always include the names of their baptized children; to ordain and install Ruling Elders and Deacons on their election by the church, and to require these officers to devote themselves to their work; to examine the records of the proceedings of the Deacons; to establish and control Sabbath schools and Bible classes, with especial reference to the children of the Church; to order collections for pious uses; to take the oversight of the singing in the public worship of God; to assemble the people for worship when there is no minister; to concert the best measures for promoting the spiritual interests of the church and congregation; to observe and carry out the lawful injunctions of the higher courts; and to appoint representatives to the Presbytery and the Synod. who shall, on their return, make report of their diligence.

VI. The Session shall hold stated meetings at least quarterly. Moreover, the Pastor has power to convene the Session when he may judge it requisite; and he shall always convene it when requested to do so by any two of the Ruling Elders; and when there is no Pastor, it may be convened by two Ruling Elders. The Session shall, also, convene when directed so to do by the Presbytery.

VII. Every Session shall keep a fair record of its proceedings, which record shall be at least once in every year submitted to the inspeetion of the Presbytery.

VIII. Every Session should keep a fair record of baptisms, of those admitted to the

Lord's table, of non-communicating members, and of the deaths and dismissions of church members.

IX. Meetings of the Session should ordinarily be opened and closed with prayer.

Section IV.—Of the Presbytery.

I. The Presbytery consists of all the Ministers and one Ruling Elder from each church within a certain district.

II. Every Ruling Elder not known to the Presbytery shall produce a certificate of his regular appointment from the Session of the church which he represents.

III. Any three Ministers belonging to the Presbytery, together with at least one Ruling Elder, being met at the time and place appointed, shall be a quorum competent to proceed to business.

IV. Ministers seeking admission to a Presbytery shall be examined on experimental religion, and also touching their views in theology and church government. If applicants come from other denominations, the Presbytery shall also require th m to answer in the affirmative the questions put to candidates at their ordination.

V. The Presbytery shall cause to be transc ibed in some convenient part of the book of records, the obligations required ot Ministers at their ordination, which shall be subscribed by all admitted to membership, in the following form. viz: ''I, A B, do *ex animo* receive and subscribe the above obligations as a just and true exhibition of my faith and principles and do resolve and promise to exercise my ministry in conformity thereunto.''

VI. The Presbytery has power to receive and issue appeals, complaints, and references brought before it in an orderly manner; to examine and license ca didates for the holy ministry; to receive, dismiss, ordain, install, remove, and judge Ministers; to review the records of church Sessions, redress whatever they may have done contrary to order, and take effectual care that they observe the Constitution of the Church; to establish the pastoral relation, and to dissolve it at the request of one or both of the parties, or where the interests of religion imperatively demand it: to set apart Evangelists to their proper work; to require Ministers to devote themselves diligently to their sacred calling, and to censure the delinquent; to see that the lawful injunctions of the higher courts are obeyed; to condemn erroneous opinions which injure the purity or peace of the Church; to visit churches for the purpose of inquiring into and redressing the evils that may have arisen in them; to unite or divide churches, at the request of the members thereof; to form and receive new churches; to take special oversight of vacant churches; to concert measures for the enlargement of the Church within its bounds; in general, to order whatever pertains to the spiritual welfare of the churches under its care; to appoint commissioners to the General Assembly; and, finally, to propose to the Synod or to the Assembly such measures as may be of common advantage to the Church at large.

VII. The Presbytery shall keep a full and fair record of its proceedings, and shall send it up to the Synod annually for review. It shall report to the Synod and the General Assembly every year the condition and progress of religion within its bounds during the year; and all the important changes which may have taken place, such as the licensures, the ordinations, the receiving or dismissing of members, the removal of members by death, the union and the division of churches, and the formation of new ones.

VIII. The Presbytery shall meet at least twice a year on its own adjournment; and when any emergency shall require a meeting sooner than the time to which it stands adjourned, the Moderator, or, in case of his absence, death, or inability to act, the Stated Clerk shall, with the concurrence, or at the request of two Ministers and two Ruling Elders of different churches, call a special meeting. For this purpose he shall give notice, specifying the particular business of the intended meeting, to every Minister belonging to the Presbytery, and to the Session of every vacant church, in due time previous to the meeting, which shall not be less than ten days. And nothing shall be transacted at such special meeting besides the particular business for which the court has been thus convened.

IX. Ministers, in good standing in other Presbyteries, or in any ecclesiastical body with which this Church has established correspondence, being present at any meeting of the Presbytery, may be invited to sit and deliberate as corresponding members. Also Ministers of like standing in other Evangelical Churches may be invited to sit as visiting brethren. In all these cases it is proper for the Moderator to introduce these Ministers to the Presbytery, and give them the right hand of fellowship.

Section V.—Of the Synod.

I. The Synod consists of all the Ministers and one Ruling Elder from each church, in a district comprising at least th e Presbyteries. The qualifications for membership in the Synod and the Presbytery are the same.

II. The Synod shall meet at least once in each year, and any seven Ministers belonging to it who shall convene at the time and place of meeting, with at least three Ruling Elders, shal be a quorum: Provided not more than three of the said Ministers belong to one Presbytery.

III. The same rule as to corresponding members, which is laid down with respect to the Presbytery, shall apply to the Synod.

IV. The Synod has power to receive and issue all appeals, complaints, and references, regularly brought up from the Presbyteries; to review the records of the Presbyteries, and redress whatever they may have done contrary to order; to take effectual care that they observe the Constitution of the Church, and that they obey the lawful injunctions of the higher courts; to erect new Presbyteries, and unite or divide those which were before erected; to appoint Ministers to such work, proper to their office, as as may fall under its own particular jurisdiction; in general, to take such order with respect to the Presbyteries, Sessions and Churches under its care as may be in conformity with the Word of God and the established rules and may tend to promote the edification of the Church, to concert measures for promoting the prosperity and enlargement of the Church within its bounds;

and, finally, to propose to the General Assembly such measures as may be of common advantage to the whole Church.

V. It shall be the duty of the Synod to keep full and fair records of its proceedings, to submit them annually to the inspection of the General Assembly. and to report to it the number of its Presbyteries, and of the members thereof, and in general, all important changes which may have occurred within its bounds during the year.

Section VI.—Of the General Assembly.

I. The General Assembly is the highest court of this Church, and represents in one body all the churches thereof. It bears the title of THE GENERAL ASSEMBLY OF THE PRESBYTERIAN CHURCH IN THE UNITED STATES, and constitutes the bond of union, peace and correspondence among all its congregations and courts.

II. The General Assembly shall meet at least annually, and shall consist of commissioners from the Presbyteries in the following proportion, viz: Every Presbytery shall be entitled to send one Minister and one Ruling Elder; but if it consists of more than twenty-four ministerial members, it shall send an additional Minister and Ruling Elder.

III. Each Commissioner, before his name shall be enrolled as a member of the Assembly, shall produce from his Presbytery a commission under the hand of the Moderator and Clerk in the following or like form, viz:

" The Presbytery of
being met at   on the
          day of   , doth

hereby appoint A. B., Minister [or Ruling Elder. as the case may be], and in case of his absence, then C. D., Minister [or Ruling Elder. as the case may be]. to be a Commissioner on behalf of this Presbytery to the next General Assembly of the Presbyterian Church in the United States, to meet at
on the　　　　　day of　　　　　A. D.,' or wherever and whenever the said Assembly may happen to sit; to consult, vote, and determine on all things that may come before that body, according to the principles and Constitution of this Church and the Word of God. And of his diligence herein he is to render an account at his return.

"*Signed by order of the Presbytery.*
(C. D.) *Clerk.*　　　　　(A. B.) *Moderator.*

IV. Any eighteen of these commissioners, of whom one-half shall be Ministers, and at least five shall be Ruling Elders. being met on the day and at the place appointed, shall be a quorum for the transaction of business.

V. The General Assembly shall have power to receive and issue all appeals, references and complaints regularly brought before it from the inferior courts; to bear testimony against error in doctrine and immorality in practice, injuriously affecting the Church; to decide in all controversies respecting doctrine and discipline; to give its advice and instruction, in conformity with the Constitution, in all cases submitted to it; to review the records of the Synods; to take care that the inferior courts observe the Constitution ; to redress whatever they may have done contrary to order: to concert measures for promoting the prosperity and enlargement of the Church; to erect new Synods; to institute and superintend the agencies necessary in the general work of evangelization; to appoint Ministers to such labors as fall under its jurisdiction; to suppress schismatical contentions and disputations, according to the rules provided therefor; to receive under its jurisdiction, with the consent of a majority of the Presbyteries, other ecclesiastical bodies whose organization is conformed to the doctrine and order of this Church; to authorize Synods and Presbyteries to exercise similar power in receiving bodies suited to become constituents of those courts, and lying within their geographical bounds respectively; to superintend the affairs of the whole Church; to correspond with other Churches; and in general. to recommend measures for the promotion of charity, truth and holiness through all the churches under its care.

VI. The whole business of the Assembly being finished. and the vote taken for dissolving the present Assembly, the Moderator shall say from the chair: "By virtue of the authority delegated to me by the Church. let this General Assembly be dissolved, and I do hereby dissolve it, and require another General Assembly, chosen in the same manner, to meet at   at on the   day of   A. D.;" after which he shall pray and return thanks. and pronounce on those present the apostolic benediction.

Section VII.—Of Ecclesiastical Commissions.

I. Commissions differ from ordinary committees, in this. that while the committee is appointed simply to examine. consider. and report, the commission is authorized to deliberate upon and conclude the business submitted to it, subject. however. to the review of the court appointing it. To this end full records of its proceeding; shall be submitted to the court appointing it, which, it approved, may be entered on the minutes of that court.

II. The taking of testimony in judicial cases, the ordination of Ministers, the installation of Ministers, the visitation of portions of the Church affected with disorder, and the organization of new churches, may be executed by commission. The commission for the ordination of a Minister shall always consist of a quorum of the court, but the Presbytery itself shall conduct the previous examinations.

III. The Synod and the General Assembly may, with the consent of parties, commit any case of trial coming before them on appeal to the judgment of a commission, composed of others than members of the court from which the appeal shall come up. The commission of a Synod shall consist of not less than fifteen, of whom seven shall be Ruling Elders; the commission of the Assembly of not less than twenty-seven, of whom thirteen shall be Ruling Elders. In each case, two-thirds of the commissioners shall be a quorum to attend to business. The commission shall try the cause in the manner prescribed by the Rules of Discipline; and in rendering judgment shall make a full statement of the case, which shall be submitted to the court for its action as its judgment in the cause.

IV. The General Assembly shall have power to commit the various interests pertaining to the general work of evangelization to one or more commissions.

CHAPTER VI.

OF CHURCH ORDERS.

Section I.—Of the Doctrine of Vocation.

I. O linary vocation to office in the Church is the calling of God by the Spirit, through the inward testimony of a good conscience, the manifest approbation of God's people, and the concurring judgment of the lawful court of Christ's house according to His Word.

II. Since the government of the Church is representative, the right of the election of their officers by God's people, either immediately by their own suffrages, or mediately through church courts composed of their chosen representatives, is indefeasible. Nor can any man be placed over a church, in any office, without the election, or at least the con sent of that church.

III. Upon those whom God calls to bear office in His Church He bestows suitable gifts for the discharge of their various duties. Wherefore every candidate for office is to be approved by the court by which he is to be ordained. And it is indispensable that, besides possessing the necessary gifts and abilities, natural and acquired, every one admitted to an office should be sound in the faith, and that his life and conversation be according to godliness.

Section II.—Of the Doctrine of Ordination.

I. Those who have been lawfully called are to be inducted into their respective offices by the ordination of a court.

II. Ordination is the authoritative admission of one duly called to an office in the Church of God, accompanied with prayer and the imposition of hands, to which it is proper to add the giving of the right hand of fellowship.

III. As every ecclesiastical office, according to the Scriptures, is a special charge, no man sha l be ordained unless it be to the performance of a definite work.

Section III.—Of the Election of Church Officers.

1. Every church shall elect persons to the offices of Pastor, Ruling Elder and Deacon in the following manner, viz: Public notice shall previously be given by the Session that the church is to convene at the usual place of public worship for such purpose : and it shall always be the duty of the Session to convene them when requested by a majority of the persons entitled to vote.

II. It is important that in all these elections a Minister should preside ; but if the Session find it impracticable. without hurtful de'ay, to procure the attendance of a Minister, tl e election may nevertheless be held.

III. The voters being convened, the Moderator shall put the question to them whether they are ready to proceed to the election. If they declare themselves ready, the Moderator shall call for nominations, after which the election shall immediately proceed, unless the electors prefer to postpone it to a subsequent day; or the e'ection may proceed by ballot without nominations. But in every case a majority of all the voters present shall be required to elect.

IV. All communicating members in good and regular standing, but no others, are entitled to vote in the election of church officers in the churches to which they are respectively attached; and when a majority of the electors cast their votes for a person for either of these offices, he shall be considered elected.

V. On the election of a Pastor, if it appear that a large minority of the voters are averse from the candidate who has a majority of votes, and cannot be induced to concur in the call, the Moderator shall endeavor to dissuade the majority from prosecuting it further: but if the electors be nearly or quite unanimous, or if the majority shall insist upon their right to call a Pastor, the Moderator in that case shall proceed to draw a call in due form, and to have it subscribed by them, certifying at the same time in writing the number and circumstances of those who do not concur in the call, all of which proceedings shall be laid before the Presbytery together with the call.

VI. The call shall be in the following or like form, viz:

The church of   , being, on sufficient grounds, well satisfied of the ministerial qualifications of you   , and having good hopes from our past experience (or knowledge) of your labors, that your ministrations in the gospel will be profitable to our spiritual interests, do earnestly call you to undertake the pastoral office in said congregation, promising you, in the discharge of your duty, all proper support, encouragement and obedience in the Lord. And that you may be free from worldly cares and avocations, we hereby promise and oblige our-

selves to pay you the sum of
in regular monthly (or quarterly, or half-
yearly, or yearly) payments, during the time
of your being and continuing the regular
Pastor of this church.

In testimony whereof we have respectively
subscribed our names this   day of
A. D.

Attested by A. B., Moderator of the Meeting.

VII. But if any church shall choose to subscribe its call by the Ruling Elders and Deacons, or by a committee, it shall be at liberty
to do so. But it shall, in such case, be fully
certified to the Presbytery by the Minister, or
other person who presided, that the persons
signing have been appointed for that purpose
by a public vote of the church; and that the
call has been, in all other respects, prepared
as above directed.

VIII. One or more commissioners shall be
appointed to present and prosecute the call
before the Presbytery.

IX. If the call be to a Minister or probationer of another Presbytery, the commissioners appointed to prosecute the call shall
produce an attested certificate from their own
Presbytery that it has been laid before that
body and found in order, and that permission
has been granted them to prosecute it before
the Presbytery to which he belongs.

*Section IV—Of the Ordination and Installation
of Ruling Elders and Deacons, and of
the Dissolution of their
Official Relations.*

I. When any person has been elected to
either of these offices, if the way be clear, and

he declare his purpose to accept, the Session shall appoint a day for his ordination.

II. The day having arrived, and the Session being convened in the presence of the church, a sermon shall be preached if convenient, after which the presiding Minister shall state in a concise manner the warrant and nature of the office of Ruling Elder, or Deacon, together with the character proper to be sustained, and the duties to be fulfilled. Having done this, he shall propose to the candidate, in the presence of the church, the following questions, viz:

1. Do you believe the Scriptures of the Old and New Testaments to be the Word of God, the only infallible rule of faith and practice?

2. Do you sincerely receive and adopt the Confession of Faith and the Catechisms of this Church, as containing the system of doctrine taught in the Holy Scriptures?

3. Do you approve of the government and discipline of the Presbyterian Church in the United States?

4. Do you accept the office of Ruling Elder (or Deacon, as the case may be) in this church, and promise faithfully to perform all the duties thereof?

5. Do you promise to study the peace, unity, edification and purity of the Church?

The Ruling Elder or Deacon elect having answered in the affirmative, the Minister shall address to the members of the church the following questions, viz:

Do you, the members of this church, acknowledge and receive this brother as a Ruling Elder (or Deacon), and do you promise to yield him all that honour, encouragement and obedience in the Lord, to which his office, according to the Word of God and the Constitution of this church, entitles him?

The members of the church having answered this question in the affirmative, by holding up their right hands, the Minister shall proceed to set apart the candidate, with prayer and the lay ng on of the hands of the Session, to the office of Ruling Elder (or Deacon, as the case may be). Prayer being ended, the members of the Session (and the Deacons, if the case be that of a Deacon) shall take the newly ordained officer by the hand, saying, in words to this eff ct: "We give you the right hand of fellowship to take part in this office with us." The Minister shall then say: "I now pronounce and declare that A. B. has been regularly elected, ordained and installed a Ruling Elder (or Deacon) in this church, agreeably to the Word of God, and according to the Constitution of the Presbyterian Church in the United States; and that as such he is entitled to all encouragement, honour, and obedience in the Lord: In the name of the Father, and of the Son, and of the Holy Ghost. Amen." After which he shall give to the Ruling Elder (or Deacon) and to the church, an exhortation suited to the occasion.

III. The offices of Ruling Elder and Deacon are perpetual; nor can they be laid aside at pleasure; nor can any person be degraded from either office but by deposition after regular trial. Yet a Ruling Elder or Deacon may, though chargeable with neither heresy nor immorality, become unacceptable in his official character to a majority of the church which he serves. In such a case, it is competent for the Session, upon application, either from the officer or from the church, to dissolve the relation. But no such application from either party shall be granted without affording to the other party full opportunity for stating objections.*

IV. When a Ruling Elder or Deacon removes permanently beyond the bounds of the church which he serves, his official relation shall be thereby dissolved, and the session shall record the fact.

V. When a Ruling Elder or Deacon who has been released from his official relation, is again elected to his office in the same or another church, he shall be installed after the above form, with the omission of ordination.

Section V.—Of the Ordination of Ministers, and the Formation and Dissolution of the Pastoral Relation.

I. No Minister or probationer shall receive a call from a church but by the permission of his Presbytery. When a call has been presented to the Presbytery, if found in order, and the Presbytery deem it for the good of the church, they shall place it in the hands of the person to whom it is addressed.

II. When a call for the pastoral services of a probationer has been accepted by him, the Presbytery shall take immediate steps for his ordination.

III. Trials for ordination, especially in a different Presbytery from that in which the candidate was licensed, shall consist of a careful examination as to his acquaintance with experimental religion; as to his knowledge of philosophy, theology, ecclesiastical history, the Greek and Hebrew languages, and such

_____
* See Rules of Discipline, Ch. VIII, ? X.

other branches of learning as to the Presbytery shall appear requisite: and as to his knowledge of the doctrine of the sacraments, and the principles and rules of the government and discipline of the Church. He shall further be required to preach a sermon before the Presbytery. The Presbytery being fully satisfied of his qualifications for the sacred office, shall appoint a day for his ordination, which ought, if practicable, to be in that church of which he is to be the pastor.

IV. The day appointed for the ordination having come, and the Presbytery being convened, a member of the Presbytery, previously appointed to that duty, shall preach a sermon adapted to the occasion. The same, or another member appointed to preside, shall afterwards briefly recite from the pulpit the proceedings of the Presbytery preparatory to the ordination; he shall point out the nature and importance of the ordinance, and endeavor to impress the audience with a proper sense of the solemnity of the transaction.

Then addressing himself to the candidate, he shall propose to him the following questions, viz:

1. Do you believe the Scriptures of the Old and New Testaments to be the Word of God, the only infallible rule of faith and practice?

2. Do you sincerely receive and adopt the Confession of Faith and the Catechisms of this Church, as containing the system of doctrine taught in the Holy Scriptures?

3. Do you approve of the government and discipline of the Presbyterian Church in the United States?

4. Do you promise subjection to your brethren in the Lord?

5. Have you been induced, as far as you know your own heart, to seek the office of the holy ministry from love to God and a sincere desire to promote His glory in the gospel of His Son?

6. Do you promise to be zealous and faithful in maintaining the truths of the gospel and the purity and peace of the Church, whatever persecution or opposition may arise unto you on that account?

7. Do you engage to be faithful and diligent in the exercise of all your duties as a Christian and a Minister of the gospel, whether personal or relative, private or public: and to endeavour by the grace of God to adorn the profession of the gospel in your conversation, and to walk with exemplary piety before the flock of which God shall make you overseer?

8. Are you now willing to take the charge of this church, agreeably to your declaration at accepting their call? And do you. relying upon God for strength, promise to discharge to it the duties of a Pastor?

V. The candidate having answered these questions in the affirmative, the presiding Minister shall propose to the church the following questions:

1. Do you, the people of this congregation, continue to profess your readiness to receive   , whom you have called to be your Pastor?

2. Do you promise to receive the word of truth from his mouth with meekness and love, and to submit to him in the due exercise of discipline?

3. Do you promise to encourage him in his labours, and to assist his endeavours for your instruction and spiritual edification?

4. And do you engage to continue to him while he is your Pastor that competent worldly maintenance which you have promised, and to furnish him with whatever you may see needful for the honour of religion and for his comfort among you?

VI. The people having answered these questions in the affirmative, by holding up their right hands, the candidate shall kneel. and the presiding Minister shall, with prayer and the laying on of the hands of the Presbytery, according to the apostolic example, solemnly set him apart to the holy office of the gospel ministry. Prayer being ended, he shall ri-e from his knees; and the Minister who presides shall first, and afterward all the members of the Presbytery in their order. take him by the right hand, saying, in words to this effect: "We give you the right hand of fellowship, to take part in this ministry with us." The Moderator shall then say: "I now pronounce and declare that A. B. has been regularly elected, ordained and installed Pastor of this congregation, agreeably to the Word of God. and according to the Constitution of the Presbyterian Church in the United States; and that as such he is entitled to all support, encouragement, honor, and obedience in the Lord. In the name of the Father, and of the Son, and of the Holy Ghost. Amen." After which the Minister presiding, or some other appointed for the purpose, shall give a solemn charge to the Pastor, and to the congregation, to persevere in the discharge of their reciprocal duties; and then by prayer recommend them both to the grace of God and His holy keeping; and finally, after singing a psalm or hymn, shall dismiss the con-

gregation with the usual blessing. And the
Presbytery shall duly record the transaction.

VII. After the installation, the heads of
families of the congregation then present, or
at least the Ruling Elders and Deacons, should
come forward to their Pastor, and give him
their right hand, in token of cordial reception
and affectionate regard.

VIII. In the *ordination* of probationers as
Evangelists, the eighth of the preceding questions shall be omitted, and the following sub·
stituted for it. viz:

Do you now undertake the work of an
Evangelist, and do you promise, in reliance
on God for strength. to be faithful in the discharge of all the duties incumbent on you as
a Minister of the Gospel of the Lord Jesus
Christ?

IX. No Presbytery shall ordain any proba·
tioner to the office of the gospel ministry,
with reference to his labouring within the
bounds of another Presbytery. but shall furnish him with the necessary testimonials. and
require him to repair to the Presbytery within
whose bounds he expects to labour, that he
may submit himself to its authority, according
to the Constitution of the Church.

X. In the installation of an ordained Minister. the following questions are to be substi-
tuted for those addressed to a candidate for
ordination, viz:

1. Are you now willing to take charge of
this congregation as their Pastor, agreeably to
your declaration at accepting its call?

2. Do you conscientiously believe and declare, as far as you know your own heart,
that, in taking upon you this charge, you are

influenced by a sincere desire to promote the glory of God and the good of the Church?

3. Do you solemnly promise that, by the assistance of the grace of God, you will endeavour faithfully to discharge all the duties of a Pastor to this congregation, and will be careful to maintain a deportment in all respects becoming a Minister of the gospel of Christ, agreeably to your ordination engagements?

XI. A congregation desiring to call a Pastor from his charge, shall, by its commissioners, represent to the Presbytery the ground on which it pleads his removal. The Presbytery having heard all the parties, may, upon viewing the whole case, either recommend them to desist from prosecuting the call, or may order it to be delivered to the Minister to whom it is addressed, with or without advice; or may decline to place the call in his hands, as it shall appear most for the peace and edification of the Church at large; or it may refer the whole matter to the next Synod for advice and direction; and no Pastor shall be translated without his own consent. If the parties are not ready to have the matter issued at the meeting then in progress, a written citation shall be given the Minister and his church to appear before the Presbytery at its next meeting, which citation shall be read from the pulpit on the Sabbath after sermon, at least two Sabbaths before the intended meeting.

XII. If the congregation, or other field of labour, to which a Minister or probationer is called, be under the jurisdiction of a different Presbytery, on his acceptance of a call he shall be furnished with the proper testimonials, and required to repair immediately to that Presbytery, in order that he may be regularly inducted into his office, according to the preceding directions.

XIII. When any Minister shall tender the resignation of his pastoral charge to his Presbytery, the Presbytery shall cite the church, as in the preceding directions, to appear by its commissioners at the next meeting, to show cause, if any it has, why the Presbytery should not accept the resignation. If the church fail to appear, or if its reasons for retaining its Pastor be deemed insufficient, his resignation shall be accepted, and the pastoral relation dissolved. If any church desires to be relieved of its Pastor, a similar process shall be observed. But whether the Minister or the church initiate proceedings for a dissolution of the relation, there shall always be a meeting of the church, called and conducted precisely in the same manner as when the call of a Pastor is to be made out.

Section VI.—Of the Licensure of Probationers for the Gospel Ministry.

I. Presbyteries shall license probationers to preach the gospel, in order that, after sufficiently trying their gifts, and receiving from the church a good report, they may, in due time, ordain them to the sacred office.

II. The trials of a candidate for licensure shall ordinarily be had by the Presbytery having jurisdiction of the church of which he is a member; but should any one find it more convenient to put himself under the care of a Presbytery at a distance from that to which he most naturally belongs, he may be received by the said Presbytery on his producing testimonials, either from the Presbytery within the bounds of which he has usually resided, or from any two Ministers of that Presbytery in good standing, of his exemplary piety and other requisite qualifications.

III. Candidates applying to the Presbytery to be licensed to preach the gospel, shall produce satisfactory testimonials of their good moral character, and of their being communicating members of the Church, in regular standing. And the Presbytery shall examine them respecting their experimental acquaintance with religion, and the motives which influence them to desire the sacred office. This examination shall be close and particular, and shall ordinarily be conducted in the presence of the Presbytery only. And it is recommended that the candidate be also required to produce a diploma of Bachelor or Master of Arts from some college or university; or at least authentic testimonials of his having gone through a regular course of learning.

IV. The Presbytery shall try each candidate as to his knowledge of the Latin language and the original languages of the Holy Scriptures. It shall also examine him on mental philosophy, logic and rhetoric; on ethics; on the natural and exact sciences; on theology, natural and revealed; and on ecclesiastical history, the sacraments, and church government. Moreover, the Presbytery shall require of him—

1. A discussion in Latin of a *thesis* on some common head in divinity.

2. An *exegesis* or *critical exercise*, in which the candidate shall give a specimen of his taste

and judgment in sacred criticism; presenting an explication of the original text, stating its connection, illustrating its force and beauties, removing its difficulties, and solving any important questions which it may present.

3. A *lecture* or exposition of several verses of Scripture.

4. A *sermon.*

V. These, or other similar exercises, at the discretion of the Presbytery, shall be exhibited until it shall have obtained satisfaction as to the candidate's piety, learning and aptness to teach in the Church.

VI. No candidate, except in extraordinary cases, shall be licensed, unless he shall have completed the usual course of academical studies, and shall also have studied divinity at least two years under some approved teacher of theology; and whenever any Presbytery shall see reason to depart from this rule, it shall always make a record of the fact upon its minutes, with the reasons therefor.

VII. If the Presbytery be satisfied with his trials, it shall then proceed to license him in the following manner: The Moderator shall propose to him the following questions, viz:

1. Do you believe the Scriptures of the Old and New Testaments to be the Word of God, the only infallible rule of faith and practice?

2. Do you sincerely receive and adopt the Confession of Faith and the Catechisms of this Church, as containing the system of doctrine taught in the Holy Scriptures?

3. Do you promise to study the peace, unity, and purity of the Church?

4. Do you promise to submit yourself, in the Lord, to the government of this Presby-

tery, or any other into the bounds of which you may be called ?

VIII. The candidate having answered these questions in the affirmative, and the Moderator having offered up a prayer suitable to the occasion, he shall address the candidate to the following purpose: " In the name of the Lord Jesus Christ, and by that authority which He has given to the Church for its edification, we do license you to preach the gospel as a probationer for the holy ministry, wherever God in His providence may call you ; and for this purpose may the blessing of God rest upon you, and the Spirit of Christ fill your heart. Amen." And record shall be 'made of the licensure in the following or like form, viz :

At   , the   day of
              , the Presbytery of
having received testimonials in favour of
                   , of his having gone through a regular course of literature, of his good moral character, and of his being in the communion of the Church, proceeded to take the usual parts of trial for his licensure. And he having given satisfaction as to his accomplishments in literature, as to his experimental acquaintance with religion, and as to his proficiency in divinity and other studies, the Presbytery did, and hereby does, express its approbation of all these parts of trial. And he having adopted the Confession of Faith and the Catechisms of this Church, and satifactorily answered the questions appointed to be put to candidates to be licensed, the Presbytery did, and hereby does, license him, the said   , to preach the gospel of Christ, as a probationer for the holy ministry, within the bounds of this Pres-

bytery, or wherever else he shall be orderly called.

IX. When any candidate for licensure shall have occasion, while his trials are going on, to remove from the bounds of his own Presbytery into those of another, it shall be considered regular for the latter Presbytery. on his producing proper testimonials from the former, to take up his trials at the point at which they were left, and conduct them to a conclusion in the same manner as if they had been commence d by itself.

X. In like manner, when any probationer, after licensure. shall by the permission of his Presbytery, remove beyond its limits, an extract of the record of his licensure, and a presbyterial recommendation, signed by the Clerk, shall be his testimonials to the Presbytery under whose care he shall come.

XI. Presbyteries should require probationers to devo e themselves diligently to the trial of their gifts; and no one should be ordained to the work of the gospel ministry until he has given evidence of his ability to edify the Church.

XII. When a probationer shall have been preaching for a considerable time, and his services do not appear to be edifying to the Church, the Presbytery may, if it thinks proper, recall his license; and it shall be its duty to do so whenever the probationer shall without necessity devote himself to such pursuits as interfere with a full trial of his gifts, according to his license.

CHAPTER VII.

OF THE CONSTITUTION OF THIS CHURCH.

I. The Constitution of the Presbyterian Church in the United States consists of its doctrinal symbols, embraced in the Confession of Faith, and the Larger and Shorter Catechisms, together with the Book of Church Order, which comprises the Form of Government, the Rules of Discipline, and the Directory of Worship.

II. The Book of Church Order may be amended on the recommendation of one General Assembly, when a majority of the Presbyteries advise and consent thereunto, and a succeeding General Assembly shall enact the same.

PART II.

THE RULES OF DISCIPLINE.

CHAPTER I.

OF DISCIPLINE—ITS NATURE, SUBJECTS, AND ENDS.

I. Discipline is the exercise of that authority, and the application of that system of laws which the Lord Jesus Christ has appointed in His Church. The term has two senses, the one referring to the whole government, inspection, training, guardianship, and control, which the Church maintains over its members, its officers, and its courts ; the other a restricted and technical sense, signifying judicial prosecution.

II. In the one sense, all baptized persons, being members of the Church, are subject to its discipline, and entitled to the benefits thereof; but in the other, it refers only to those who have made a profession of their faith in Christ.

III. The ends of discipline, as it involves judicial prosecution, are the rebuke of offences, the removal of scandal, the vindication of the honour of Christ, the promotion of the purity and general edification of the Church, and the spiritual good of offenders themselves.

IV. The power which Christ has given to the rulers of His Church is for edification, and not for destruction; it is a dispensation of mercy, and not of wrath. As in the preaching of the word the wicked are doctrinally separated from the good, so by discipline the Church authoritatively separates between the holy and the profane. In this it acts the part of a tender mother, correcting her children fo their good, that every one of them may b presented faultless in the day of the Lord Jesus.

CHAPTER II.

OF THE DISCIPLINE OF NON-COMMUNICATING MEMBERS.

I. The oversight of the children of the Church is committed by God primarily to believing parents, who are responsible to the Church for the faithful discharge of this duty The responsibility of parents continues during the minority of their children, and extends to all such conduct contrary to the purity and sobriety of the gospel as parents may and ought to restrain and control.

II. The Church should make special provision for the instruction of its youth in the doctrines of the Bible as set forth in the Catechisms. Hence, Church Sessions ought to establish, under their own authority, Bible classes and Sabbath schools for this object, or

to adopt such other methods as shall secure
the same end.

III. When the children of the Church arrive
at years of discretion, they are bound to discharge all the duties of church members. If
they give evidence of saving faith in Christ,
together with a correct walk and conversation,
they should be informed that it is their privi·
lege and duty to make a profession of faith in
Christ, and to come to His table. If they exhibit a wayward disposition, and associate
themselves with the profane, the Church
should still cherish them in faith, and ought
to use all such means as the Word of God
warrants and the christian prudence of church
officers shall dictate, for reclaiming them and
bringing them to appreciate their covenant
privileges, and to discharge their covenant
obligations.

IV. Those adult non-communicating members who submit with meekness and gratitude
to the government and instruction of the
Church, are entitled to special attention.
Their rights under the covenant should be
frequently and fully explained and their duties enforced on their consciences; they should
be warned of the sin and danger of neglecting
their covenant obligations, and urged by the
mercies of Christ to come up to their full discharge.

V. All non-communicating members shall
be deemed under the care of the church to
which their parents belong, if they live under
the parental roof and are minors; or otherwise, under that of the church where they re-
side, or with which they ordinarily worship.

CHAPTER III.

OF OFFENCES.

I. An offence, the proper object of judicial process, is anything in the principles or practice of a church member professing faith in Christ, which is contrary to the Word of God. The Confession of Faith and the Larger and Shorter Catechisms of the Westminster Assembly, together with the formularies of government, discipline, and worship, are accepted by the Presbyterian Church in the United States as standard expositions of the teachings of Scripture in relation to both faith and practice. Nothing, therefore, ought to be considered by any court as an offence. or admitted as a matter of accusation, which cannot be proved to be such from Scripture. as interpreted in these standards.

II. Offences are either personal or general, private or public; but all of them being sins against God, are, therefore grounds of discipline.

III. Personal offences are violations of the Divine law, considered in the special relation of wrongs or injuries to particular individuals. General offences are heresies or immorralities. having no such relation, or considered apart from it.

IV. Private offences are those which are known only to a few persons. Public offences are those which are notorious.

CHAPTER IV.

OF CHURCH CENSURES.

I. The censures which may be inflicted by church courts are, admonition, suspension, excommunication, and deposition. When a lower censure fails to reclaim the delinquent, it may become the duty of the court to proceed to the infliction of a higher censure.

II. Admonition is the formal reproof of an offender by a church court, warning him of his guilt and danger, and exhorting him to be more circumspect and watchful in the future.

III. Suspension, with respect to church members, is their temporary exclusion from sealing ordinances; with respect to church officers, it is their temporary exclusion from the exercise of their office. It may be either definite or indefinite as to its duration. Definite suspension is administered when the credit of religion, the honour of Christ, and the good of the delinquent demand it, even though he may have given satisfaction to the court. Indefinite suspension is the exclusion of an offender from sealing ordinances, or from his office, until he exhibit signs of repentance, or until, by his conduct, the necessity of the highest censure be made manifest.

IV. Excommunication is the excision of an offender from the communion of the Church. This censure is to be inflicted only on account of gross crime or heresy, when the offender shows himself incorrigible and contumacious. The design of this censure is to operate on the offender as a means of reclaiming him, to deliver the Church from the scandal of his offence, and to inspire all with fear by the example of his discipline.

V. Deposition is the degradation of an officer from his office, and may or may not be accompanied with the infliction of other censure.

CHAPTER V.

OF THE PARTIES IN CASES OF PROCESS.

I. Original jurisdiction in relation to Ministers of the Gospel pertains exclusively to the Presbytery, and in relation to other church members to the Session.

II. It is the duty of all church Sessions and Presbyteries to exercise care over those subject to their authority ; and they shall, with due diligence and great discretion, demand from such persons satisfactory explanations concerning reports affecting their Christian character. This duty is more imperative when those who deem themselves aggrieved by injurious reports shall ask an investigation. If such investigation, however originating, should result in raising a strong presumption of the guilt of the party involved, the court shall institute process, and shall appoint a prosecutor to prepare the indictment, and to conduct the case. This prosecutor shall be a member of the court, except that, in a case before the Session, he may be any communicating member of the same congregation with the accused.

III. The original and only parties in a case of process are the accuser and the accused. The accuser is always the Presbyterian Church in the United States, whose honour and purity are to be maintained. The prosecutor, whether voluntary or appointed, is always the representative of the Church, and as such has all its rights in the case. In appellate courts the parties are known as appellant and appellee.

IV. Every indictment shall begin : " In the name of the Presbyterian Church in the United States," and shall conclude, ''against the peace, unity and purity of the Church, and the honour and majesty of the Lord Jesus Christ as the King and Head thereof." In every case the Church is the injured and accusing party, *versus* the accused.

V. An injured party shall not become a prosecutor of personal offences without having previously tried the means of reconciliation, and of reclaiming the offender, required by Christ : " Moreover, if thy brother shall trespass against thee, go and tell him his fault between thee and him alone : if he shall hear thee, thou hast gained thy brother ; but if he will not hear thee, then take with thee one or two more, that in the mouth of two or three witnesses every word may be established." Matt. xviii : 15, 16. A church court, however, may judicially investigate personal offences as if general, when the interests of religion seem to demand it, So, also, those to whom private offences are known cannot become prosecutors, without having previously endeavoured to remove the scandal by private means.

VI. When the offence is general, the cause

may be conducted either by any person appearing as prosecutor, or by a prosecutor appointed by the court.

VII. When the prosecution is instituted by the court, the previous steps required by our Lord in the case of personal offences are not necessary. There are many cases, however, in which it will promote the interests of religion to send a committee to converse in a private manner with the offender, and endeavour to bring him to a sense of his guilt, before instituting actual process.

VIII. Great caution ought to be exercised in receiving accusations from any person who is known to indulge a malignant spirit towards the accused; who is not of good character; who is himself under censure or process; who is deeply interested in any respect in the conviction of the accused; or who is known to be litigious, rash, or highly imprudent.

IX. Every voluntary prosecutor shall be previously warned, that if he fail to show probable cause of the charges, he must himself be censured as a slanderer of the brethren, in proportion to the malignity or rashness manifested in the prosecution.

X. When a member of a church court is under process, all his official functions may be suspended, at its discretion: but this shall never be done in the way of censure.

XI. In the discussion of all questions arising in his own case, the accused shall exercise the rights of defendant only, not of judge.

CHAPTER VI.

OF GENERAL PROVISIONS APPLICABLE TO ALL CASES OF PROCESS.

I. It is incumbent on every member of a court of Jesus Christ, engaged in a trial of offenders, to bear in mind the inspired injunction: "If a man be overtaken in a fault, ye which are spiritual restore such an one in the spirit of meekness, considering thyself, lest thou also be tempted."

II. Process against an offender shall not be commenced unless some person or persons undertake to make out the charge; or unless the court finds it necessary, for the honour of religion, itself to take the step provided for in chapter V., paragraph II.

III. When a charge is laid before the Session or Presbytery, it shall be reduced to writing, and nothing shall be done at the first meeting of the court, unless by consent of parties, except to appoint a prosecutor, and order the indictment to be drawn, a copy of which, with the witnesses then known to support it, shall be served on the accused, and to cite all parties and their witnesses to appear and be heard at another meeting, which shall not be sooner than ten days after such citation; at which meeting of the court the charges shall be read to the accused, if present, and he shall be called upon to say whether he be guilty or not. If he confess, the court may deal with him according to its discretion; if he plead and take issue, the trial shall proceed. Accused parties may plead in writing, when they cannot be personally present, and parties necessarily absent should have counsel assigned to them.

IV. The citation shall be issued and signed by the Moderator or Clerk, by order and in the name of the court; he shall also issue citations to such witnesses as either party shall nominate to appear on his behalf.

V. In drawing the indictment, the times, places and circumstances should, if possible, be particularly stated, that the accused may have full opportunity to make his defence.

VI. When an accused person shall refuse to obey a citation, he shall be cited a second time; and this second citation shall be accompanied with a notice that if he do not appear at the time appointed (unless providentially hindered, which fact he must make known to the court), or that if he appear and refuse to plead, he shall be dealt with for his contumacy, as hereinafter provided.

VII. The time which must elapse between the serving of the first citation on the accused person, and the meeting of the court at which he is to appear, shall be at least ten days. But the time allotted for his appearance on the subsequent citation, shall be left to the discretion of the court; provided that it be not less than is quite sufficient for a seasonable and convenient compliance with the citation.

VIII. When the offence with which an accused person stands charged took place at a distance, and it is inconvenient for the witnesses to appear before the court having jurisdiction, that court may either appoint a commission of its body, or request the co-ordinate court contiguous to the place where the facts occurred, to take the testimony for it. The accused shall always have reasonable notice of the time and place of the meeting of this commission.

IX. When an offence, alleged to have been committed at a distance, is not likely otherwise to become known to the court having jurisdiction, it shall be the duty of the court within whose bounds the facts occurred, after satisfying itself that there is probable ground of accusation, to send notice to the court having jurisdiction, which shall at once proceed against the accused ; or the whole case may be remitted for trial to the co-ordinate court within whose bounds the offence is alleged to have been committed.

X. Before proceeding to trial, courts ought to ascertain that their citations have been duly served.

XI. In every process, if deemed expedient, there may be a committee appointed, which shall be called the Judicial Committee, and whose duty it shall be to digest and arrange all the papers, and to prescribe, under the direction of the court, the whole order of the proceedings. The members of this committee shall be entitled, notwithstanding their performance of this duty, to sit and vote in the case as members of the court.

XII. When the trial is about to begin, it shall be the duty of the Moderator solemnly to announce from the chair that the court is about to pass to the consideration of the cause, and to enjoin on the members to recollect and regard their high character as judges of a court of Jesus Christ, and the solemn duty in which they are about to engage.

XIII. In order that the trial may be fair and impartial, the witnesses shall be examined in the presence of the accused, or at least after he shall have received due citation to attend. Witnesses may be cross-examined by both parties, and any questions asked which are pertinent to the issue.

XIV. On all questions arising in the progress of a trial, the discussion shall first be between the parties; and when they have been heard they may be required to withdraw from the court, until the members deliberate upon and decide the point.

XV. When a court of first resort proceeds to the trial of a cause, the following order shall be observed: 1. The Moderator shall charge the court. 2. The indictment shall be read, and the answer of the accused heard. 3. The witnesses for the prosecutor, and then those for the accused, shall be examined. 4. The parties shall be heard, first the prosecutor, and then the accused, and the prosecutor shall close. 5. The roll shall be called, that the members may express their opinion in the cause. 6. The decision shall be made, and judgment entered on record.

XVI. Either party may, for cause, challenge the right of any member to sit in the trial of the case, which question shall be decided by the members of the court, other than the one challenged.

XVII. Pending the trial of a cause, any member of the court who shall express his opinion of its merits to either party, or to any person not a member of the court; or who shall absent himself from any sitting without the permission of the court, or satisfactory reasons rendered, shall be thereby disqualified from taking part in the subsequent proceedings.

XVIII. The parties shall be allowed copies

of the whole proceedings, at their own ex-
pense, if they demand them. Minutes of the
trial shall be kept by the clerk, which shall
exhibit the charges. the answer, all the testimony, and all such acts, orders, and decisions
of the court relating to the cause, as either
party may desire, and also the judgment.
The clerk shall, without delay, attach together the charges, the answer. the citations and
returns thereto, and the minutes herein required to be kept. These papers, when so
attached, shall constitute "the record of the
cause." When a cause is removed by appeal
or complaint, the lower court shall transmit
"the record" thus prepared to the higher
court, with the addition of the notice of appeal or complaint, and the reisons thereof, if
any shall have been fi'ed. Nothing which is
not contained in this "record" shall be taken into consideration in the higher court. On the
final decision of a cause in a higher court, its
judgment shall be sent down to the court in
which the case originated.

XIX. No professional counsel shall be per-
mitted as such to appear and plead in cases of
process in any court; but an accused person
may, if he desires it, be repre-ented before
the Session by any communicating member
of the same particular church; or before any
other court, by any member of the court. A
member of the court so employed shall not
be allowed to sit in judgment in the cause.

XX. Process, in case of scandal, shall commence within the space of one year after the
offence was committed, unless it has recently
become flagrant. When, however, a church
member shall commit an offence, after removing to a place far distant from his former resi-

dence, and where his connection with the Church is unknown, in consequence of which circumstances process cannot be instituted within the time above specified, the recent discovery of the church membership of the individual shall be considered as equivalent to the offence itself having recently become flagrant. The same principle in like circumstances, shall also apply to Ministers.

CHAPTER VII.

SPECIAL RULES PERTAINING TO PROCESS BEFORE SESSIONS.

I. Process against all church members, other than Ministers of the gospel, shall be entered before the Session of the church to which such members belong.

II. When an accused person, having been twice duly cited, shall refuse to appear before the Session, or appearing, shall refuse to plead, the court shall enter upon its records the fact, together with the nature of the offence charged, and he shall be suspended from sealing ordinances for his contumacy. This sentence shall be made public, and shall in no case be removed until he has not only repented of his contumacy, but has given satisfaction in relation to the charges against him.

III. If the charge be one of gross crime or heresy, and the accused persist in his contumacy, the court may proceed to inflict the highest censure.

IV. When it is impracticable immediately to

comence process against an accused church member. the Session may, if it think the edification of the Church require it, prevent the accused from approaching the Lord's table, until the charges against him can be examined.

————

CHAPTER VIII.

SPECIAL RULES PERTAINING TO PRŌCESS AGAINST A MINISTER.

I. Process against a Minister shall be entered before the Presbytery of which he is a member.

II. As no Minister ought, on account of his office, to be screened in his sin, or slightly censured, so scandalous charges ought not to be received against him on slight grounds.

III. If any one know a Minister to be guilty of a private offence, he should warn him in private. But if the offence be persisted in, or become public, he should bring the case to the attention of some other Minister of the Presbytery for his advice.

IV. If a Minister accused of an offence, having been twice duly cited, shall refuse to appear before the Presbytery, he shall be immediately suspended. And if. after another citation, he still refuse to attend, he shall be deposed as contumacious, and suspended or excommunicated from the Church. Record shall be made of the judgment and of the charges under which he was arraigned, and the sentence shall be made public.

V. Heresy and schism may be of such a nature as to warrant deposition; but errors ought to be carefully considered, whether they strike at the vitals of religion, and are industriously spread, or whether they arise from the weakness of the human understanding, and are not likely to do much injury.

VI. If the Presbytery find on trial that the matter complained of amounts to no more than such acts of infirmity as may be amended, so that little or nothing remains to hinder the Minister's usefulness, it shall take all prudent measures to remove the scandal.

VII. When a Minister, pending a trial, shall make confession, if the matter be base and flagitious, such as drunkenness, uncleanness, or crimes of a higher nature, however penitent he may appear to the satisfaction of all, the court shall, without delay, suspend him from the exercise of his office, or depose him from the ministry.

VIII. A Minister suspended or deposed for scandalous conduct, shall not be restored, even on the deepest sorrow for his sin, until he shall exhibit for a considerable time such an eminently exemplary, humble, and edifying walk and conversation as shall heal the wound made by his scandal. And a deposed Minister shall in no case be restored until it shall appear that the general sentiment of the Church is strongly in his favour, and demands his restoration; and then only by the court inflicting the censure, or with its consent.

IX. When a Minister is deposed his church shall be delared vacant; but when he is suspended, it shall be left to the discretion of the Presbytery whether the sentence shall include the dissolution of the pastoral relation.

X. Whenever a Minister of the gospel shall habitually fail to be engaged in the regular discharge of his official functions, it shall be the duty of the Presbytery, at a stated meeting, to inquire into the cause of such dereliction, and if necessary, to institute judicial proceedings against him for breach of his covenant engagement. If it shall appear that his neglect proceeds only from his want of acceptance to the Church, Presbytery may, upon the same principle upon which it withdraws license from a probationer for want of evidence of the Divine call, divest him of his office without censure, even against his will, a majority of two-thirds being necessary for this purpose.

In such a case, the clerk shall, under the order of the Presbytery, forthwith deliver to the individual concerned a written notice that, at the next stated meeting, the question of his being so dealt with is to be considered. This notice shall distinctly state the grounds for this proceeding. The party thus notified shall be heard in his own defence ; and if the decision pass against him, he may appeal, as if he had been tried after the usual forms.

This principle may apply, *mutatis mutandis,* to Ruling Elders and Deacons.

CHAPTER IX.

OF EVIDENCE.

I. All persons of proper age and intelligence are competent witnesses, except such as do not believe in the existence of God, or a future state of rewards and punishments. The accused party may be allowed, but shall not be compelled, to testify; but the accuser shall be required to testify on the demand of the accused. Either party has the right to challenge a witness whom he believes to be incompetent, and the court shall examine and decide upon his competency. It belongs to the court to judge of the degree of credibility to be attached to all evidence.

II. A husband or wife shall not be compelled to bear testimony the one against the other in any court.

III. The testimony of more than one witness shall be necessary in order to establish any charge; yet if, in addition to the testimony of one witness, corroborative evidence be produced, the offence may be considered to be proved.

IV. No witness afterwards to be examined except a member of the court, shall be present during the examination of another witness on the same case, if either party object.

V. Witnesses shall be examined, first by the party introducing them; then cross-examined by the opposite party; after which any member of the court, or either party, may put additional interrogatories. But no question shall be put or answered, except by permission of the Moderator, subject to an appeal to the court; and the court shall not permit questions frivolous or irrelevant to the charge at issue.

VI. The oath or affirmation to a witness shall be administered by the Moderator in the following or like terms: "You solemnly promise. in the presence of God. that you will declare the truth, the whole truth, and nothing but the truth, according to the best of your knowledge in the matter in which you are called to witness, as you shall answer it to the great Judge of quick and dead." If. however, at any time a witness should present himself before a court, who, for conscientious reasons, prefers to swear or affirm in any other manner, he shall be allowed to do so.

VII. Every question put to a witness shall, if required. be reduced to writing. When answered. it shall, together with the answer, be recorded, if deemed by the court, or by either party, of sufficient importance, and the testimony of the witness shall be read to him for his approbation and subscription.

VIII. The records of a court, or any part of them, whether original or transcribed. if regularly authenticated by the Moderator and Clerk, or by either of them, shall be deemed good and sufficient evidence in every other court.

IX. In like manner, testimony taken by one court and regularly certified, shall be received by every other court, as no less valid than if it had been taken by itself.

X. When it is not convenient for a court to have the whole, or perhaps any part of the testimony in a particular cause, taken in its presence, a commission shall be appointed to take the testimony in question, which shall be considered as if taken in the presence of the court; of which commission, and of the time and place of its meeting, due notice shall be given to the opposite party, that he may have an opportunity of attending. And if the accused shall desire, on his part, to take testimony at a distance, for his own exculpation, he shall give notice to the court of the time and place at which it is proposed to take it, that a commission, as in the former case, may be appointed for the purpose. Or, the testimony may be taken on written interrogatories, by filing the same with the clerk of the court having jurisdiction of the cause, and giving two weeks' notice thereof to the adverse party, during which time he may file cross-interrogatories if he desire it; and the testimony shall then be taken by the commission in answer to the direct and cross-interrogatories, if such are filed, and no notice need be given of the time and place of taking the testimony.

XI. A member of the court shall not be disqualified for sitting as a judge by having given testimony in the case.

XII. An officer or private member of the church refusing to testify, may be censured for contumacy.

XIII. If, after a trial before any court, new testimony be discovered, which is supposed to be highly important to the exculpation of the accused, it is proper for him to ask, and for the court to grant, a new trial.

XIV. If, in the prosecution of an appeal, new testimony be offered, which, in the judgment of the appellate court, has an important bearing on the case, it shall be competent for that court to refer the cause to the inferior court for a new trial; or, with the consent of parties, to take the testimony and proceed with the cause.

CHAPTER X.

OF THE INFLICTION OF CHURCH CENSURES.

I. Ecclesiastical censures ought to be suited to the nature of the offence; for private offences censures shonld be administered in the presence of the court alone, or privately, by one or more members on its behalf; but for public offences, censures should be administered in open session, or publicly announced to the church. When there are peculiar and special reasons, the court may visit public offences, not very gross in their character, with private admonition, or with definite suspension in private; but the censure of indefinite suspension should ordinarily be announced to the church, whilst those of excommunication and deposition should be either administered before the church, or else announced to it, at the discretion of the court.

II. When any member or officer of the Church shall be guilty of a fault deserving censure, the court shall proceed with all tenderness, and shall deal with its offending brother in the spirit of meekness, the members considering themselves, lest they also be tempted.

III. The censure of admonition ought to be administered in private, by one or more members, in behalf of the court, when the offence is not aggravated, and is known only to a few. When the scandal is public, the admonition shall be administered by the Moderator in the presence ot the court, and ordinarily shall also be announced in public.

IV. Definite suspension being an exemplary censure, ought ordinarily to be either administered in open session, or announced to the church.

V. The censure of indefinite suspension ought to be inflicted with great solemnity, that it may be the means of impressing the mind of the delinquent with a proper sense of his danger, while he stands excluded from the sacraments of the Church of the living God, and that with the Divine blessing it may lead him to repentance. When the court has resolved to pass this sentence, the Moderator shall address the offending brother to the following purpose :

" WHEREAS, You, A. B. (here describe the person as a Minister, Ruling Elder, Deacon, or private member of the Church), are convicted by sufficient proof [or, are guilty by your own confession], of the sin of —— (here insert the offence), we, the Presbytery [or church Session] of C. D., in the name and by the authority of the Lord Jesus Christ, do now declare you suspended from the sacraments of the Church [and from the exercise of your office], until you give satisfactory evidence of repentance."

To this shall be added such advice or admonition as may be judged necessary, and the whole shall be concluded with prayer to Almighty God that He would follow this act of discipline with His blessing.

VI. When the sentence of excommunication has been regularly passed, the Moderator of the Session shall make a public statement before the church of the several steps which have been taken with respect to their offending brother, and inform them that it has been found necessary to cut him off from the communion of the Church. He shall then show the authority of the Church to cast out unworthy members, from Matt. xviii : 15-18, and 1 Cor. v : 1-5, and shall explain the nature, use and consequence of this censure, warning the people, that they are to conduct themselves, in all their intercourse with him as is proper towards one who is under the heaviest censure of the Church. He shall then pronounce sentence to the following effect :

"WHEREAS, A B, a member of this church, has been, by sufficient proof, convicted of the sin of ———, and after much admonition and prayer, obstinately refuses to hear theChurch, and has manifested no evidence of repentance: Therefore, in the name and by the authority of the Lord Jesus Christ, we, the Session of the church of C. D., do pronounce him to be excluded from the sacraments, and cut off from the fellowship of the Church."

After which prayer shall be made that the blessing of God may follow His ordinance, for the conviction and reformation of the excommunicated, and for the establishment of all true believers.

VII. The sentence of deposition shall be pronounced by the Moderator, in words of the following import :

" WHEREAS, A. B.. a Minister of this Presbytery [or a Ruling Elder or Deacon of this church]. has been proved, by sufficient evidence, to be guilty of the sin of ———, we, the Presbytery [or Church Session], of C. D., do adjudge him totally disqualified for the office of the Christian Ministry [or Eldership, or Deaconship], and therefore we do hereby, in the name and by the authority of the Lord Jesus Christ, depose from the office of a Christian Minister [or Elder, or Deacon], the said A. B., and do prohibit him from exercising any of the functions thereof." If the sentence include suspension or excommunication, the Moderator shall proceed to say: "We do moreover, by the same authority, suspend the said A. B. from the sacraments of the Church, until he shall exhibit satisfactory evidence of sincere repentance," or "exclude the said A. B. from the sacraments, and cut him off from the fellowship of the Church."

The sentence of deposition ought to be inflicted with solemnities similar to those already prescribed in the case of excommunication.

CHAPTER XI.

OF THE REMOVAL OF CENSURES.

I. After any person has been suspended from the sacraments, it is proper that the rulers of the church should frequently converse with him, as well as pray with him, and for him, that it would please God to give him repentance.

II. When the court shall be satisfied as to the reality of the repentance of a suspended offender, he shall be admitted to profess his repentance, either in the presence of the court alone, or publicly, and be restored to the sacraments of the Church, and to his office, if such be the judgment of the court, which restoration shall be declared to the penitent in words of the following import :

"WHEREAS, You, A. B., have been debarred from the sacraments of the Church [and from the office of the gospel Ministry, or Eldership, or Deaconship], but have now manifested such repentance as satisfies the church, we, the Session (or Presbytery) of C. D., do hereby, in the name and by the authority of the Lord Jesus Christ, absolve you from the said sentence of suspension, and do restore you to the full enjoyment of sealing ordinances. [and the exercise of your said office, and all the functions thereof.]"

After which there shall be prayer and thanksgiving.

III. When an excommunicated person shall be so affected with his state as to be brought to repentance, and to desire to be readmitted to the communion of the Church, the Session, having obtained sufficient evidence of his sincere penitence, shall proceed to restore him. In order to which, the presiding Minister shall inform the church of the measures which have been taken with the excommunicated person, and of the resolution of the Session to restore him.

On the day appointed for his restoration, the Minister shall call upon the excommunicated person, and propose to him in the presence of the congregation the following questions :

"Do you from a deep sense of your great wickedness, freely confess your sin in thus rebelling against God, and in refusing to hear

His Church; and do you acknowledge that you have been in justice and mercy cut off from the communion of the Church? *Answer.* —I do. Do you now voluntarily profess your sincere repentance and contrition for your sin and obstinacy ; and do you humbly ask the forgiveness of God and His Church? *Answer.*—I do. Do you sincerely promise, through divine grace, to live in all humbleness of mind and circumspection ; and to endeavor to adorn the doctrine of God our Savior, by having your conversation as becometh the gospel? *Answer.*—I do.''

Here the minister shall give the penitent a suitable exhortation, encouraging and comforting him. Then he shall pronounce the sentence of restoration in the following words :

"Whereas, you, A. B., have been shut out from the communion of the Church, but have now manifested such repentance as satisfies the Church ; in the name of the Lord Jesus Christ, and by His authority, we, the Session of this church, do declare you absolved from the sentence of excommunication formerly denounced against you; and we do restore you to the communion of the Church, that you may be a partaker of all the benefits of the Lord Jesus to your eternal salvation."

The whole shall be concluded with prayer and thanksgiving.

IV. The restoration of a deposed officer, after public confession has been made in a manner similar to that prescribed in the case of the removal of censure from an excommunicated person, shall be announced to him by the Moderator in the following form, viz :

"Whereas, you, A. B., formerly a Minister

of this Presbytery, [or a Ruling Elder or
Deacon of this church,] have been deposed
from your office, but have now manifested
such repentance as satisfies the Church ; in
the name of the Lord Jesus Christ, and by
His authority, we, the Presbytery of C. D.,
[or the Session of this church,] do declare
you absolved from the said sentence of deposition formerly pronounced against you ; and
we do furthermore restore you to your said
office, and to the exercise of all the functions
thereof, whenever you may be orderly called
thereto."

After which there shall be prayer and
thanksgiving, and the members of the court
shall extend to him the right hand of fellowship.

V. When an Elder or Deacon has been
absolved from the censure of deposition, he
can not be allowed to resume the exercise of
his office in the church without re-election by
the peop'e.

VI. When a person under censure shall
remove to a part of the country remote from
the court by which he was sentenced, and
shall desire to profess repentance and obtain
restoration it shall be lawful for the court,
if it deem it expedient, to transmit a certified
copy of its proceedings to the Session (or
Presbytery) where the delinquent resides,
which shall take up the case, and proceed
with it as though it had originated with
itself.

VII. In proceeding to restore a suspended
or deposed Minister. it is the duty of the Presbytery to exercise great caution : first admit-
ting him to the sacraments, if he has been
debarred from the same, afterwards granting

him the privilege of preaching for a season on probation, so as to test the sincerity of his repentance and the prospect of his usefulness; and finally restoring him to his office. But the case shall always be *sub judice* until the sentence of restoration has been pronounced.

CHAPTER XII.

OF CASES WITHOUT PROCESS.

I. When any person shall come forward and make his offence known to the court, a full statement of the facts shall be recorded, and judgment rendered without process.

II. When a communicating member shall confess before the church Session an unregenerate heart, and there is no evidence of other offence, the court may transfer his name to the roll of non-communicating members, and he shall be faithfully warned of his guilt in disobeying the gospel, and encouraged to seek the redemption freely offered in Christ ; and a statement of the case shall be made to the church. But this action shall not be taken until the church Session has ascertained, after mature inquiry and due delay, that this confession does not result from Satanic temptation or transient darkness of spirit. This rule, however, shall not be applied to those who wilfully absent themselves from the Lord's table, which is always an offence.

III. A Minister of the gospel, against whom

there are no charges, if fully satisfied in his own conscience that God has not called him to the ministry, or if he has satisfactory evidence of his inability to serve the Church with acceptance, may report these facts at a stated meeting. At the next stated meeting, if after full deliberation the Presbytery shall concur with him in judgment, it may divest him of his office without censure, and shall assign him membership in some particular church.

IV. When a member or officer shall renounce the communion of this Church by joining some other evangelical Church, if in good standing, the irregularity shall be recorded, and his name erased. But if charges are pending against him, they shall be communicated to the Church which he has joined. If the denomination be heretical, an officer shall have his name stricken from the roll, and all authority to exercise his office derived from this Church shall be withdrawn from him; but a private member shall not be otherwise noticed than as above prescribed.

CHAPTER XIII.

OF THE MODES IN WHICH A CAUSE MAY BE CARRIED FROM A LOWER TO A HIGHER COURT.

I. Every decision which is made by any church court, except the highest, is subject to the review of a superior court, and may be brought before it by general review and control, reference. appeal, or complaint.

II. When a matter is transferred in any of these ways from an inferior to a superior court, the members of the inferior court shall not lose their right to sit, deliberate, and vote in the case in the higher courts. except that either of the original parties may challenge the right of any members of the inferior court to sit, which question shall be decided by the vote of all those members of the superior court who are not members of the inferior.

Section I—Of General Review and Control.

I. It is the duty of every court above a church Session, at least once a year, to review the records of the proceedings of the courts next below. And if any lower court shall omit to send up its records for this purpose. the higher court may issue an order to produce them, either immediately, or at a particular time, as circumstances may require.

II. In reviewing the records of an inferior court, it is proper to examine. *First,* Whether the proceedings have been constitutional and regular ; *Secondly,* Whether they have been wise, equitable, and for the edification of the

Church; *Thirdly*, Whether they have been correctly recorded; *Fourthly*, Whether the lawful injunctions of the superior courts have been obeyed.

III. In most cases the superior court may be considered as fulfilling its duty by simply recording on its own minutes the approval, the correction of proceedings, or the censure which it may think proper to pass on the records under review; and also by making an entry of the same in the book reviewed. But should any irregular proceedings be found such as demand the interference of the superior court, the inferior court may be required to review and correct them.

IV. In cases of process, however, no judgment of an inferior court shall be reversed, unless it be regularly brought up by appeal or complaint.

V. Courts may sometimes entirely neglect to perform their duty, by which neglect heretical opinions, or corrupt practices may be allowed to gain ground; or offenders of a very gross character may be suffered to escape; on some circumstances in their proceedings of very great irregularity may not be distinctly recorded by them; in any of which cases their records will by no means exhibit to the superior court a full view of their proceedings. If, therefore, the next superior court be well advised that any such neglect or irregularity has occurred on the part of the inferior court, it is incumbent on it to take cognizance of the same and to examine, deliberate and judge in the whole matter as completely as if it had been recorded, and thus brought up by the review of the records.

VI. When any court having appellate jurisdiction shall be advised, either by the records of the court next below, or by memorial, either with or without protest, or by any other satisfactory method, of any important delinquency or grossly unconstitutional proceedings of such court, the first step shall be to cite the court alleged to have offended to appear by representative or in writing, at a specified time and place, and to show what it has done or failed to do in the case in question. The court thus issuing the citation may reverse or redress the proceedings of the court below in other than judicial cases; or it may censure the delinquent court; or it may remit the whole matter to the delinquent court, with an injunction to take it up and dispose of it in a constitutional manner; or it may stay all further proceedings in the case, as circumstances may require.

VII. In process against an inferior court, the trial shall be conducted according to the rules provided for process against individuals, so far as they may be applicable.

Section II.—Of References.

I. A reference is a representation of a matter not yet decided, made by an inferior to a superior court, which representation ought always to be in writing.

II. Cases which are new, important, difficult or of peculiar delicacy, the decision of which may establish principles or precedents of extensive influence; on which the sentiments of the inferior court are greatly divided; or on which, for any reason, it is desirable that a superior court should first decide, are proper subjects for reference.

III. References are either for mere advice, preparatory to a decision by the inferior court ; or for ultimate decision by the superior court.

IV. In the former case, the reference only suspends the decision of the court from which it comes ; in the latter, it submits the whole case to the final judgment of the superior court.

V. Although references may, in some cases, be proper, yet it is, generally, conducive to the good of the Church that every court should fulfil its duty by exercising its judgment.

VI. A reference ought, generally, to procure advice from the superior court, yet that court is not bound to give a final judgment, but may remit the whole case, either with or without advice, to the court by which it was referred.

VII. References by any court are to be made to the court immediately superior,

VIII. When a court makes a reference, it ought to have all the testimony and other documents duly prepared, produced, and in perfect readiness, so that the superior court may be able to consider and issue the case with as little difficulty or delay as possible.

Section III,—Of Appeals.

I. An appeal is the removal of a cause, already decided, from an inferior to a superior court, the effect of which is to arrest sentence until the matter is finally decided. It is allowable only after judgment has been rendered, and to the party against whom the decision has been rendered.

II. Those who have not submitted to a

regular trial are not entitled to appeal.

III. Any irregularity in the proceedings of the inferior court; a refusal of reasonable indulgence to a party on trial; declining to receive important testimony; hurrying to a decision before the testimony is fully taken; a manifestation of prejudice in the cause; and mistake or injustice in the judgment, are all proper grounds of appeal.

IV. Every appellant is bound to give notice of his intention to appeal, and also to lay the reasons thereof in writing before the court appealed from, either before its rising or within ten days thereafter. If this notice or these reasons be not given to the court while in session, they shall be lodged with the Moderator or Clerk.

V. No appeal shall be carried from an inferior to any other court than the one immediately superior, without its consent.

VI. The appellant shall lodge his appeal, and the reasons of it, with the Clerk of the higher court before the close of the second day of its sessions; and the appearance of the appellant and appellee shall be either in person or by writing.

VII. In taking up an appeal, after ascertaining that the appellant on his part has conducted it regularly, the first step shall be to read "the record of the cause;" the second, to hear the parties, first the appellant, then the appellee, and the appellant shall close; the third, to call the roll, that the members may express their opinion in the cause; and then the vote shall be taken.

VIII. The decision may be either to confirm or reverse, in whole or in part, the judgment of the inferior court; or to remit the cause for the purpose of amending the record; should it appear to be incorrect or defective, or for a new trial.

IX. If an appellant, after entering his appeal to a superior court, fail to prosecute it, it shall be considered as abandoned, and the judgment appealed from shall be final. And an appellant shall be considered as abandoning his appeal if he do not appear before the appellate court by the second day of its meeting next ensuing the date of his notice of appeal, unless it shall appear that he was prevented by the providence of God from seasonably prosecuting it.

X. If an appellant is found to manifest a litigious or other unchristian spirit in the prosecution of his appeal, he shall be censured according to the degree of his offence.

XI. If the infliction of the sentence of suspension, excommunication or deposition be arrested by appeal, the judgment appealed from shall nevertheless be considered as in force untill the appeal shall be issued.

XII. If any court shall neglect to send up the record of the cause, especially if thereby an appellant who has proceeded with regularity shall be deprived of the privilege of having his appeal seasonably tried, it shall be censured according to the circumstances of the case, and the judgment appealed from shall be suspended until the record be produced, upon which the issue can be fairly tried.

Section IV.—Of Complaints.

I. A complaint is a representation made to a superior court against an inferior court. Any member of the Church, submitting to its authority, may complain against every species of decision, except where a party, against whom a decision has been rendered, takes his appeal against it. But the complaint shall not suspend, while pending, the effect of the decision complained of.

II. Notice of complaint shall be given in the same form and time as notice of appeal.

III. The parties to a complaint shall be denominated complainant and respondent; and the latter shall be the court against which the complaint is taken. After the superior court has ascertained that the complaint is regular, its first step shall be to read "the record" of the case; its second, to hear the complainant; its third, to hear the respondent by its representative; its fourth, to hear the complainant again; and then it shall consider and decide the case.

IV. The superior court has discretionary power either to annul any portion or the whole of the decision complained of, or to send it back to the inferior court with instructions for a new hearing.

V. The court against which complaint is taken is bound to send up its records in the case, as hereinbefore provided.

CHAPTER XIV.

OF DISSENTS AND PROTESTS.

I. A dissent is a declaration on the part of one or more members of a minority in a court, expressing a different opinion from that of the majority in a particular case. A dissent unaccompained with reasons shall be entered on the records of the court.

II. A protest is a more solemn and formal declaration by members of a minority bearing their testimony against what they deem a mischievous or erroneous judgment, and is generally accompanied with a detail of the reasons on which it is founded.

III. If a protest or dissent be couched in temperate language, and be respectful to the court, it shall be recorded; and the court may, if deemed necessary, put an answer to the protest on the records along with it. But here the matter shall end, unless the parties protesting obtain permission to withdraw their protest absolutely, or for the sake of amendment.

IV. None can join in a protest against a decision of any court, except those who had a right to vote in the case.

CHAPTER XV.

OF JURISDICTION.

I. When any member shall remove from one church to another, he shall produce satisfactory testimonials of his church-membership and dismission before he be admitted as a regular member of that congregation, unless the church Session has other satisfactory means of information.

II. When a church member or officer shall remove his residence beyond the bounds of the court to whose jurisdiction he belongs into the bounds of another, it he shall neglect for twelve months, without satisfactory reasons given to both these courts, to transfer his ecclesiastical relations, the court whose bounds he has left shall be required to transfer them. And should that court neglect this duty, the one into whose bounds he has removed shall assume jurisdiction, giving due notice to the other body.

III. Members of one church dismissed to join another shall be held to be under the jurisdiction of the Session dismissing them, till they form a regular connection with that to which they have been dismissed.

IV. If the residence of a communicating member be unknown for three years, he shall be retired upon a separate roll until he shall reappear and give satisfaction; of which due record shall be made.

V. When a Presbytery shall dismiss a minister, probationer or candidate, the name of the Presbytery to which he is dismissed shall be given in the certificate, and he shall remain under the jurisdiction of the Presbytery dismissing him, until received by the other.

VI. No certificate of dismission, from either a Session or a Presbytery, shall be valid testimony of good standing for a longer period than one year, unless its earlier presentation be hindered by some providential cause; and such certificates given to persons who have left the bounds of the Session or Presbytery granting them, shall certify the standing of such persons only to the time of their leaving those bounds.